Alfons Wolff

Über das gemeinrechtliche Prinzip der Regulirung der Beweislast

Beweislast

Alfons Wolff

Über das gemeinrechtliche Prinzip der Regulirung der Beweislast

ISBN/EAN: 9783743647312

Hergestellt in Europa, USA, Kanada, Australien, Japan

Cover: Foto ©Suzi / pixelio.de

Weitere Bücher finden Sie auf **www.hansebooks.com**

DR FLINT'S SERMON

ON THE

DEATH OF DR ABBOT.

A

SERMON,

DELIVERED IN THE MEETING-HOUSE

OF THE

FIRST PARISH OF BEVERLY,

JUNE 18, 1828,

ON THE OCCASION OF THE LAMENTED DEATH

OF THE

REV. ABIEL ABBOT, D. D.

LATE PASTOR OF THE FIRST CHURCH AND SOCIETY IN BEVERLY.

Second Edition.

BY JAMES FLINT, D. D.

MINISTER OF THE SECOND CHURCH AND SOCIETY IN SALEM.

SALEM,

PUBLISHED BY J. R. BUFFUM.

1828.

V

.

-

,

50 Washington Street,
ISAAC R. BUTTS AND CO.'S PRESS.

REVEREND AND DEAR SIR,

THE undersigned beg leave to express to you the thanks of the Members of the First Parish in Beverly, for the Sermon delivered by you in consequence of the death of DR ABBOT, in which you so beautifully and happily delineated the mind and character of their late much esteemed and beloved Pastor, and kind and devoted friend,—and would request of you the favor of a copy for the press.

We are, very respectfully,

Dear Sir, your obedient servants,

THOMAS DAVIS,
ROBERT RANTOUL,
WILLIAM THORNDIKE,
JOSIAH LOVETT,
SAMUEL P. LOVETT,
Committee of Arrangements.

REV. DR FLINT.

SALEM, JUNE 20, 1828.

GENTLEMEN,

I FEEL no other hesitation in complying with the request so kindly expressed in your note, than is prompted by my regret that the hasty tribute I was called to pay, in much weakness, to the memory of your " late much esteemed and beloved Pastor, and kind and devoted friend," falls so far short of the worth and distinguished endowments of its dear and lamented subject ; such, however, as it is, I submit it to your disposal.

I am, with unfeigned respect, gentlemen,

Your obedient servant,

JAMES FLINT.

Messrs THOMAS DAVIS, and others,
Committee of Arrangements.

To the bereaved family and flock of the deceased, the following Sermon is inscribed, with the affectionate sympathy and respects of

THE AUTHOR.

SALEM, JUNE 20, 1828.

SERMON.

1. Thessalonians, iv. 13. *Sorrow not even as others which have not hope,——the hope laid up for you in heaven.* Colossians, i. 5.

My Christian Friends,

It is no rare occurrence for a bereaved individual or mourning family to appear within these walls. Today, we have come together, at the call of a mysterious Providence, one entire assembly of mourners, to mingle our tears, our sympathies and prayers, as partakers in a common calamity,—to render our united tribute of merited honor to the memory of a revered servant of God, and to express our unavailing regret for the loss of a highly gifted and faithful minister of Jesus Christ, sorrowing most of all,—not for him, for we know that it is well with the righteous, and that the dead are blessed, who die in the Lord,—but for ourselves, that we shall see his face no more in the flesh.

One mournful and affecting image is present to the thoughts of all,—that of the good shepherd of this bereaved flock and the honored head of this afflicted family fallen the untimely victim of disease, at the moment when recruited health had given promise of lengthened years of usefulness and peace in the bosom of his beloved charge and household. The aspect of universal sadness and grief, which I see before me occasioned by this event, admonishes me, that you deplore with no common feeling of bereavement, the unlooked for summons of your religious monitor, guide, counsellor and friend to his early rest and reward, leaving you, as it has pleased God he should, to mourn over the sudden prostration of hopes, that had been so recently raised almost to the certainty of fruition. The husband and parent, in whom were centred the dearest earthly interests and tenderest affections of a fondly cherished and devoted family, has been denied to the arms already extended to embrace him. The pastor, so long and dearly prized by his expecting anxious flock, has been arrested by death, while hurrying with eager haste to lead them once more, as he trusted, beside the still waters and in green pastures, and to have his joy fulfilled in their joy at his return to them with renovated strength, and in the fulness of the blessing of the Gospel of Christ. The voice, to which you had expected once more to have listened the last Sabbath in this place, which has here so often raised your hearts to God and so often soothed the sorrows of the mourner, is now hushed in the long silence of the grave. The ear that hath heard him shall hear him no more. The eye that hath seen him shall see him no more. The places that have known him shall know him no more. You have not had even the melancholy satisfaction of rendering the last offices to his insensible dust, and of placing it in the sacred enclosure, in which you had all hoped, that it might have reposed in its last sleep with yours.

It is a common weakness of our nature to associate all our recollections of the departed with the body, even when the spirit that animated it is gone, as our religion assures us, to mingle with kindred spirits in glorified bodies fashioned like unto that of our glorified Saviour. And it is, therefore, no small addition to the pain of bereavement, when the loved form of the friend we mourn is laid in a distant grave,—when

> " By foreign hands his dying eyes were closed,
> By foreign hands his lifeless limbs composed,
> By foreign hands his lonely grave adorn'd,
> By strangers honor'd, and by strangers mourn'd."

The death of a neighbor, or a casual acquaintance, in the obscurest walks of life, brings a shade of sadness and solemnity over the mind of the most unreflecting and unconnected witness of the event. But God speaks to us with a louder warning and more solemn emphasis, when the eminent and the good are taken away, who have long filled a large space in the public regard, and sustained the most responsible relations that exist in human society. A thousand common objects may, we know, be removed out of their place without attracting the notice of many observers. But the sudden disappearance of a lighthouse or watchtower, that had long stood, as a guide to the mariner, or the traveller, cannot take place without awakening a general interest and at-

tention. And if, as we have all so of ten seen and
felt, the impression be slight and transient, when the
living read the lesson of their frailty in the frequent
funerals of the promiscuous crowd of all ages, whose
existence and exit are alike unknown beyond their
immediate vicinity, it is not so, it cannot be so, when
death has selected, as in the instance we mourn, an
elevated and shining mark, and, by removing with a
stroke, a distinguished individual, has deprived not
only a family of its dearest earthly dependence and
solace, but a numerous and united people of their
spiritual father, and the visible centre and bond of
their union; the church and commonwealth of a pil-
lar and an ornament; his brethren in the ministry of
a brother whose presence was to them as the light
of the morning, whose friendship and hearty counsel
have so often rejoiced their hearts, given ardor to
their zeal, wisdom and elevation to their purposes,
and imparted a charm, a sweet and hallowing influence, to their intercourse on earth, the remembrance of which they will love to cherish, while
they live, as an earnest of the higher and dearer
communion which they hope to share with him in
heaven.

It is to this hope, laid up for us in heaven, and to
the consoling remembrances associated with the life
and labors and character of him we mourn, that all,
who partake in the sorrows of this occasion, must
turn for relief from those painful feelings which the
peculiarly afflictive circumstances of the event we
deplore are calculated to produce and prolong;
and upon which we have already dwelt, as we are

naturally prone to dwell, with a pertinacity of mournful remembrance and regret, perhaps not meet to be indulged by those who believe that not a sparrow falls to the ground without the knowledge and direction of our Father in heaven, and who profess to confide in the promise which he has promised us by his Son, even eternal life. Think then no more of these circumstances, except to acknowledge that they have been ordered by a better wisdom than ours. Let reason, let piety repress the wanderings of that "busy meddling memory," that loves to bring before the mind melancholy images, which wound and depress the spirit, without making the heart better. Forget the place and manner, in which the spirit of the good and faithful servant received its summons to enter into the joy of his Lord. It is of small moment to him who holds himself always in readiness to depart, whether he expire at home or abroad, in the bosom of his family, or among strangers, in his bed or in the open air, on the dry land or whelmed in the ways of the deep, suddenly or lingeringly. Death to him in any circumstances is infinite gain. Our sorrow is selfish, or it is an infirmity, to which Christians should be superior, if we persist to mourn, when we have just cause to believe that the departed has exchanged a corruptible for an incorruptible body, and is now clothed with immortality, shining with a splendor surpassing that of the sun and the brightness of the firmament, already entered upon his celestial progress from glory to glory in improvement and happiness without interruption or end.

If we believe such a change, a scene of such surpassing glory and transcendant joy, as is promised to them that have turned many souls to righteousness, has opened upon the soul of the beloved servant of God, who has left the scene of his labors and discipline with us upon earth, why should we mourn,—why sorrow like those who are ignorant of *the hope laid up for them in heaven?* Because the voice to which you once listened with delight is silent to you, would you recall it from mingling in the songs of the blessed, that it might instruct and gladden you again only for a few short years? Because God has changed the countenance that once beamed with affection on you, and has now made it radiant in his presence with the light and glory which shall hereafter be revealed in all his children, would you, if you might, divest it of the image of the heavenly, that you might see it again bear the image of the earthly man, even though his face, like that of the blessed martyr, might be to you as the face of an angel? Did you, while the faithful pastor, the good father, and the bosom friend was with you, sincerely wish his happiness, his peace, his joy, and that he might be shielded from pain and sorrow? How inconsistent then your grief for his removal. The words of Jesus, when he said, *in this world ye shall have tribulation*, have been verified in the experience of all his servants. The christian ministry has been significantly likened to the little book in the apocalypse, " a bitter sweet, and the sweet comes first;" and in every relation of this checkered scene of mingled good and evil,

there can be no security against suffering, no pledge
or guarantee of continued happiness. But in the
world to which we trust in Jesus Christ our brother
is gone, all is security, rest, unchangeable serenity and
fulness of joy ; for there *the spirits of the just are made
perfect; they have entered into life, neither can they
die any more ; for they are equal unto the angels, and
are the children of God, being the children of the resurrection. The wicked is driven away in his wicked-
ness; but the souls of the righteous are in the hands
of God, and there shall no torment touch them. In
the sight of the unwise they seemed to die; and their
departure was taken for misery, and their going from
us to be utter destruction ; but they are in peace. And
I heard a voice from heaven, saying unto me, write,
Blessed are the dead which die in the Lord from hence-
forth ; Yea, saith the spirit, that they may rest from
their labors, and their works do follow them.*

Why, then, regret their departure ? Happy for
them, nay, happy for us, that no tears or prayers
can bring them back again. The truer, the intenser
our love for them, the more truly and fervently shall
we thank God, that it is not permitted us to recall
them. For we may adopt, in respect to our departed brother, the language of one, who felt as a Christian should feel upon this subject,—

——" what here we call our life is such,
So little to be loved, and thou so much,
We should but ill requite thee to constrain
Thy unbound spirit into bonds again."

The departed cannot return to us ; but we shall ere
long, and may soon go to them. All the living are

following in solemn procession the generations that have gone before; and the entire human race, from the beginning to the end of time, appears in the eyes of Him who liveth for ever, but one vast funeral train, moving in perpetual succession to the grave, and there putting off this mortal to be clothed with immortality. • *For as with Adam all die, so with Christ shall all be made alive. For since by man came death, so by man also has come the resurrection of the dead.*

To the mansions of the blessed, whither our virtuous progenitors and kindred have preceded us,—whither your departed pastor so often and affectionately besought you all with prayers and many tears to raise with him your views and affections, and

> ——" tried each art, reproved each dull delay,
> Allured to brighter worlds and led the way"—

to those happy mansions, the way is open to all who will ask and seek and strive to go up thither; and your pastor now beseeches you by the awful eloquence of the grave, to enter in. *Come up hither* is the united voice of all that dwell with God, and of God himself, to you that survive. Obey this voice; *gird up the loins of your minds, be sober and watch unto prayer;* and death that has divided you from your pastor and friend for a season, will rejoin you to him, each in your turn; and as he hails and welcomes your successive arrival thither, until you are all gathered into the fold of the great shepherd and bishop of souls, not one wanderer lost, then will he *rejoice in the day of Christ, that he*

has not run in vain, neither labored in vain. Then
will be accomplished the object of his labors, exhorta-
tions, and prayers for you. Think. then, at all times,
that you hear that well-known voice, as you have
so often heard it within these walls, addressing to you,
*not in words which man's wisdom teacheth, but in words
which the holy ghost teacheth,* which he loved to use,—
hear him, I say, addressing to you the desire which
he felt for you strong in life and in death, and which
death cannot have weakened, *that every one of you
do show the same diligence to the full assurance of
hope unto the end ; that ye be not slothful, but followers of them, who through faith and patience are gone
to inherit the promises;* for so a mansion shall be
prepared for you in your Father's house, where,
united in love with all the good and excellent of the
earth, who have lived or shall live, you shall cele-
brate together an eternal triumph over sin and death,
over sorrow and mourning, for ever holy, for ever
happy.

In view of this exceeding great and eternal weight
of glory, which constitutes *the hope laid up in heav-
en* for the Christian, and in which the good minister
of Jesus Christ, and all who are of like spirit with
him are to find their reward, not of debt, but of
God's free, rich, unbought, exuberant grace, the
apostle might well exhort us not to sorrow for those
who have fallen asleep in Jesus.

It is fit that you should remember, and that you
should never cease to remember affectionately, ten-
derly, religiously, the messenger and servant of the
Lord, who has so long been in and out before you

and shown unto you the way of salvation. God has willed that *the righteous shall be had in everlasting remembrance.* Cherishing the memory of your pastor with a grateful love, that shall dwell upon his virtues, and the lessons of piety, benevolence and peace, which fell so persuasively from his lips, and which were expressed still more eloquently in his life, will be at the same time to cherish *the hope laid up for you in heaven.* For they can hardly fail to be inseparably associated in your minds. They will mutually suggest each other. When you think of him, you will think of the bright abode of his rest, of the community of the blessed, to which you trust the God, whom he loved and served, has received him, and of the evangelical faith, life and temper by which alone he taught you to hope for an entrance into that abode, for admission to that community.

It is indeed a peculiar privilege of the minister of religion, who has been faithful, that his image is embalmed and perpetuated in the affectionate remembrance of his people by the sacred and imperishable nature of the relation he sustains to them. Unlike all the other social and various civil relations, that subsist among men, and which have respect only to *things seen and temporal*, this has respect chiefly to *things unseen and eternal.* The bonds, which bind the christian pastor to his charge and his charge to him, are "not flesh and blood, *but faith and love, that are in Christ Jesus.*" These regard the spirit that is in man, and like that are commensurate with all future duration. Heroes, patriots, statesmen, may rear higher monuments, and fill with a louder blast the clarion of fame in this world, than the humble minister of Jesus Christ. But he will have a monument, a name and a praise in the souls he has assisted in rescuing from sin and forming to holiness, which will survive when the monuments and memorials of earthly glory, and the earth itself shall have passed away. These souls will then be his crown, his glory and his joy in the presence of the Lord Jesus. And while those, who have grown up, *and been enlightened and tasted the good word of God* under his ministry, shall survive, he will continue to be remembered by them with the Sabbaths which they spent with him in beholding the beauty of the Lord and inquiring in his temple,— with the prayers in which they united with him,— with the seasons of refreshment from the presence of the Lord at his table, which they have enjoyed with him,—with the many precious gone by hours, in which they took sweet counsel together, mingled mind with mind, and heart with heart, upon themes, which will be of everlasting interest to them, and which they will take up anew and pursue together in the light and communion of eternity.

Few ministers have left more and better founded claims to be thus remembered than our excellent and lamented brother. And I would, for the honor of our common faith and ministry, which he so recommended and adorned by the daily beauty of his life, that I were endowed with a portion of his rare gifts to do justice to these claims. But this is an ambitious wish, which I must repress, and resign the task to some other mind of kindred discrimination, delicacy of tact, and felicity of painting with his own. I must be content to advert briefly to a few particulars of his history, and to arrest, while they are fresh in our minds, a few recollections of the minister and man, as we have known him.

Dr Abbot seems to have been endowed by nature and early culture with a singular combination of qualities peculiarly adapted to the ministry. It is not every educated and even talented youth, however sober and exemplary, from which can be made a good minister, any more than from every piece of wood the statuary can shape out a Mercury. It requires a harmony and proportion of development in the several intellectual and moral powers, in which no single one predominates, so as to over-shadow and dwarf the growth and vigor of the rest. Very splendid talents are apt to generate in the possessor a pride of intellect, and thirst for notoriety, hardly compatible with the meekness of wisdom, which should characterize the minister of Jesus. A man thus extraordinarily endowed, instead of contenting himself with being the humble and faithful organ for dispensing and enforcing the plain truths and simple yet sublime instructions of his master, is prone to deal in theories and speculations, in refinements, abstractions, and generalizations beyond the reach of the common mind, which, however they may evince his own genius and intellectual power, exhibit very little of the genius of Christianity, or that *wisdom of God and power of God, which is unto salvation to every one that believeth.* If a

man possess a strong aptitude for excellence in the
exercise of some particular mental faculty,—has, as
we say, a genius for logic, a genius for criticism,
an imaginative mind, or a metaphysical mind, the
master faculty, whatever it may be, obtrudes itself
in all his intellectual efforts, on all occasions; and
he thinks more of displaying the peculiar gifts, in
which he excels, than of dispensing in simplicity,
and in a manner adapted to the understandings and
wants of his charge, the manifold riches of Christ,
and declaring to them the whole counsel of God,
and keeping back nothing that is profitable for doctrine, reproof, correction, and instruction in righteousness. A passion for the fame of scholarship,
or literary distinction, exerts an equally sinister influence upon the mind of a minister ; as it produces
a morbid and irritating solicitude about the estima-
tion in which his performances may be held by
judges of literary merit.

Dr Abbot's mind does not appear to have been
affected by any of these impediments to ministerial
excellence. His was a well-balanced mind. Though
possessed of fine powers, he was not ambitious of
the name of a genius ; but was satisfied with the
consciousness of consecrating his gifts to the glory
of the Giver in the able and faithful discharge of the
functions of the sacred office, which was the object
of his early predilection.

Like most of the ministers of New England, who
have sustained the piety of her churches, and adorned their office by the sanctity of their manners, Dr
Abbot was reared in a family, distinguished, as were

3

generally our yeomanry of the last century, by the
simplicity, frugality and religious order of their domestic economy. From the daily example of his
parents, and especially the instructions of a discreet
and pious mother, the aspirations of his young heart
were early directed in cheerful devotion to his Father in heaven. As all children should be taught
to do,

> " He walked with God in holy joy
> While yet his days were few ;
> The deep glad spirit of the boy
> To love and reverence grew."

And the genial flame of devotion, thus early kin-
dled at the domestic altar, and nurtured by the gentle
breathings of maternal love, was afterwards sustained and strengthened by the unfailing nutriment
which it derived from an enlightened contemplation
of the works and religious observation of the
providence of God, and still more from the habitual
study of the scriptures. He was eminently a devout
man through life ; and was remarkably, beyond most
of his brethren, as it is often expressed, gifted in
prayer. The readiness and pertinency, with which
he adapted his devotions to occasions and emer-
gencies will be long remembered in our churches.

His youthful piety accompanied him, as the guar-
dian of his innocence through his collegiate course,
in which the quickness of his parts and the facility
with which he mastered the regular studies of his
class, never tempted him to relax into indolence, or
to abuse his leisure in any sort of dissipation. He
passed that perilous ordeal of youthful virtue with-

out stain or censure, and graduated with honors
among the most distinguished of his class.   He
soon after engaged as assistant instructer in the
Academy of his native town, where, with the minister of the place, the late Rev. Jonathan French,
he pursued his theological studies, till he began to
preach at the age of twenty-four. He, from the
first, took rank among the most popular preachers
of the day. He, a short time after, received and
accepted a unanimous call to settle in Haverhill, a
beautiful village on the west bank of the Merri-
mack.

After eight years usefully and happily spent with
an affectionate people, to whom he was extremely
endeared, inadequate support and a growing family
rendered it an imperative duty, as it seemed to him,
reluctantly to ask a separation from a beloved people.   It was with equal reluctance granted.   He
immediately became a candidate for resettlement;
and of several invitations from highly respectable
societies, he gave the preference to yours.   And
here, "in the chosen spot," as he writes in his last
letter to his family, "where my tabernacle has now
been twenty-four years pitched," *ye are witnesses,
and God also, how holily and justly and unblame-
ably he has exercised his ministry among you; and
as ye also know, has exhorted and comforted and
charged every one of you, as a father doth his children, that ye would walk worthy of God, who hath
called you to his kingdom and glory.*

It is a grateful consideration, that in reviewing the
character and ministry of your pastor, you have no

obliquities of temper, no eccentricities of conduct, no extravagancies of doctrine or opinion to excuse or lament in him. There was nothing harsh or repulsive in his creed, or his manners. And how should there be, when one was modelled from the instructions, and the other from the character of him who bore the appellation of the Lamb of God, and on whom the spirit of heaven rested under the symbol of a dove? He deemed it no sin against any law of God, or the example of his master, to be a gentleman; I do not mean of the school of Chesterfield, as of hypocrisy, as of deceit, *but as of sincerity, as of God,*—of the school of St Paul, who exhorts a minister to *be gentle towards all men,* to be courteous, to become, as far as in uprightness he may, all things to all men.

There was an amenity and benignity in Dr Abbot's air and voice and address, exceedingly conciliating to strangers and endearing to his friends. His countenance beamed with complacency, and bespoke that inward satisfaction and peace,

" Which goodness bosoms over."

He had always something kind and courteous to say to every one, into whose company he fell even for a few moments; and no one could long remain in his society, that had a heart, who did not feel that he had been conversing with a man equally amiable, intelligent and gifted. The minister and the man were never in him at variance with each other. In his most playful moods there was no unbecoming levity. His sport was the innocence of a child, seasoned with the wit of man, and guarded by the circumspection of a Christian.

Of his religious sentiments it is enough to say, that he called no man master, that he belonged to no sect but that of good men,—to no school but that of Jesus Christ, and that he was liberal in the best sense of the term. Though he loved, like the eloquent preacher whose words I quote, " to escape the narrow walls of a particular church, and to stand under the open sky, in the broad daylight, looking far and wide, seeing with his own eyes, hearing with his own ears," still he never thought himself called upon to denounce the opinions of others, and rarely to obtrude his own upon the controverted points of the day. He preached, as he thought his master would have him, *speaking* what, after diligent and prayerful inquiry, he conceived to be *the truth in love.*

The publications of Dr Abbot are numerous and valuable. They all bear the stamp of a mind early imbued with the savor of classical studies, familiar with the best models of the English pulpit, enriched by observation and reflection, and fertile in apt and beautiful illustrations,—a mind susceptible of deep and lively impressions from all that is bright and fair and lovely and magnificent in creation,—a mind which had found treasures untold in the scriptures, and in which *dwelt the words of Christ richly in all wisdom,* whence he drew expressions and images that gave richness and weight to his discourses and writings, and often reminded his hearer or reader of Solomon's similitude *of words fitly spoken to apples of gold in pictures of silver;* but what is best of all, they evince a mind always intent upon doing good, and which loved and sought, uttered and enforced truth only as it appeared to him to be conducive to goodness.

Dr Abbot was *an eloquent man,* as well as *mighty in the scriptures.* If Jehovah sent Aaron to communicate his will to Pharaoh, *because he could speak well,* Dr Abbot possessed this credential of his office in an eminent degree. His manner in the pulpit was singularly impressive, grave, natural, solemn;

> " much impressed
> Himself, as conscious of his awful charge,
> And mainly anxious, that the flock he fed
> Might feel it too; affectionate in look,
> And tender in address, as well becomes
> A messenger of grace to guilty men."

He exhibited a beautiful union of zeal with prudence; and the love of souls so evidently dictated his admonitions and reproofs to the delinquent, that his fidelity and plainness seldom gave offence. In the sick chamber and in the house of mourning, he was truly *a son of consolation.*

Few men have lived more endeared, or more deservedly dear in the more private relations of life. Like all virtuous men, he sought and found the best happiness which this world affords, in the bosom of domestic affection, in the reciprocation of those sacred charities and daily offices of love, which render home, the fireside of a christian and well ordered family, at once the best emblem of the mansions

which await the righteous in our Father's house in
heaven, and the best scene of preparation for those
mansions. The yearnings of his heart to return to
this asylum of his repose, of his purest affections
and joys, are affectingly expressed on his arrival
from Cuba at Charleston : " happy am I to touch
natal soil again, and hope soon to revisit *home,
sweet home.*" *

I remark one trait more, in these days of ines-
timable value in a minister ; his signal love of peace.
No object was dearer to his heart than to bring
ministers and the people to feel on this subject, as
he felt. His convention sermon, the delivery of
which was almost the last public act of his ministry,
will now seem to his brethren, to the community,
and still more to his flock, like the dying bequest of
Jesus to his disciples ; *Peace I leave with you , my
peace I give unto you ; not as the world giveth,
give I unto you.*" No ; the world, and I grieve to
say it, the ministers of the Prince of peace, too many of them, speak a very different language, and
breathe a very different spirit. But with that dying
appeal of your pastor in your hands, you, my brethren of this ancient and respectable society, will feel
yourselves inexcusable in the sight of heaven, if you
allow discord to arise among you, or division to scat-
ter you. How much he was grieved by the angry
disputes of the day, and the rending of churches and
societies, of which they are the cause, appears in
the following extract from the letter before cited.

* The burden of a well known popular song.

" Yesterday was the anniversary of my peace sermon before the Convention. I fear its gentle notes
have not been echoed this year. There is no one
thing, that gives me so much pain in returning to
my loved country, as to think of its religious dis-
sensions. May the God of peace hush them; and
for ever preserve my voice from the notes of discord." Happy spirit, thy voice never uttered the
notes of discord, and they can never again reach
thy ear. Thou art now joined to the sons of peace,
the children of God,

> " Who have no *discord* in their song,
> Nor winter in their year."

Farewell, faithful servant of God ; thy warfare is
accomplished, thy work is finished, and thy reward
is sure. O God, with whom do rest the spirits of
just men made perfect, grant that we, who survive,
may *gird up the loins of our minds,—be sober and
watch unto prayer,—*that by diligence and persever-
ance in well doing, we *may be followers of them, who
through faith and patience, are now inheriting the
promises.* AMEN. .

APPENDIX.

Extract from a discourse delivered by Rev. JOHN BARTLETT, at Beverly, before the First Church and Society, June 22, 1828, being the first Sabbath on which religious services were performed by said Church and Society, after the death of their pastor, Rev. Dr ABBOT, was known to them.—TEXT—Acts xi. 24.—"*He was a good man, and full of the Holy Ghost, and of faith, and much people was added unto the Lord.*"

After describing the character and rewards of " a *good man*," the whole was thus applied :—

" Do you still ask for patterns to imitate, in which you may see all the parts of a holy and virtuous character beautifully illustrated ? Do you ask for the example of one, in whose daily intercourse, in whose domestic, social and public relations, in fine in whose whole life, you may see the elements and the evidences of a good man ? To whom could I more justly and pertinently refer you than to that eminent, venerated and endeared individual, by whose recent and sudden death, a beloved family are bereaved of their glory, of the best and kindest of earthly friends ; an affectionate people of a learned, faithful, tender and devoted pastor ; the churches of Christ, of one, who has always felt a lively interest in their welfare, sympathised in their sufferings, counselled and sustained them in their trials, aided and rejoiced in their prosperity ;—and his brethren in the ministry, of one, who was ever ready to the offices of love, by whose prompt sympathy and aid, by whose counsels and friendship, their labors and solitude were lightened, and by whose example, their zeal was animated to new efforts in the service of God and mankind. To be taken away from those, for whom he seemed to live, at a time too when they were eagerly expecting his return ; and when he appeared particularly desirous, and peculiarly qualified to benefit and bless society by his instructions and labors, is one of those events, which it hath pleased God to leave involved in that mystery, for the removal of which we must be willing to wait till we shall cease to ' *see through a glass darkly.*' ' *He taketh*

4

away,' says Job : *'who can hinder him ?'* There is, however, much left us of this estimable friend, which calls for devout gratitude. There are left, his character, his example, his counsels ; and there are offered to us what were his consolations, and what we believe is now his reward. *' Blessed are the dead who die in the Lord,'* &c. &c. It is not my intention to sketch his biography. This requires a pen of happier power than any I can bring. All that I can present is the tribute of friendship and gratitude. You all knew him. He was ever among you, as your pastor, your friend and brother. You have seen and felt his worth. And is it not to be hoped, that to many of you his instructions have been a *savour of life unto life ?* How clear and pursuasively were they given. How fraught with meaning ; how enlivened by beautiful and apt metaphor, and enforced by sound argument. How mighty was he in the Scriptures, and how pertinent in his application of them. With what fervency and benevolent solicitude were your interests commended by him to the Father of mercies ; and how affectionately and earnestly did he always exhort you, like Barnabas, *to cleave to the Lord with full purpose of heart.* Surely *' he was a good man and full of the holy ghost and of faith,'* and it is believed that by him *'much people were added to the Lord.'*

" I would, on this occasion, forbear indulging personal feelings of friendship, by attempting to portray all the excellences of his private character. I shall narrate only one circumstance, which, *now,* I feel that I have not the liberty to conceal ;—a circumstance which illustrates his piety and faithfulness ; his preparedness for death, and the justice of applying to his character the words of the text. On a visit to him, made at his request, a few days before his departure to a warmer climate, for the benefit of his health ; at a time when his physician and friends and he himself were apprehensive, that the disease, which then oppressed him, would speedily terminate his life ; at this time, when the heart has no disguise, and the soul is anxious to utter all that it deems true and kind, important and useful, he thus addressed me (evidently with a wish that it should be remembered and at a fit time communicated)—' I believe the hour of my departure is at hand ; how near I cannot say, but not far distant is the time when I shall be in the immediate presence of my Maker. This impression leads me to look back upon my life and inwardly upon my present state. In the review I find many things to be humbled and penitent for, and many things to fill me with gratitude and praise. I have, I trust, the testimony of my heart, that my life, my best powers, my time, and my efforts, have in the main been sincerely given to God and to mankind. Of all the years of my life, the present, in the review, gives me most pleasure. You know my recent plans and labors, and the design of them, [alluding to discourses, delivered before the convention of ministers, and at the ordination of Rev. A. Abbot, and to certain contributions to a religious publication, the Christian Visitant, whose object coincided with his views, and to extend the circulation of which he was making great efforts.] In these, I have endeavored to check the spirit of contention among Christians, and as a disciple of the Prince of Peace, to diffuse the spirit of love and peace, to inspire Christians with a warmer zeal for the great object of religion. The efforts were great. My health and perhaps my life are the sacrifice. If the Lord will, be it so. If ever I faithfully served him, it was in these services. If ever I felt prepared for death, it was when they were finished. If ever I knew and felt the delightful import of that passage,—*I am now ready to be offered and the time of my departure is at hand; I have fought a good fight, I have finished my course, I have kept the faith*, &c, it was then, and it is now. In my own bosom there is peace. Whether life or death be before me, all is well. I can say, *the will of the Lord be done*. With the greatest serenity he alluded to the expected issue of his disorder, and seemed filled with *a good hope through grace* of eternal life. He was indeed *ready to be offered*, and is now removed, we believe, to a higher sphere, and to nobler employments and joys.

" My Brethren, he was not alone in his departure. The spirit of his near and valued friend* was, by a remarkable coincidence dismissed nearly at the same hour from the cares and duties and sufferings of this life, and called to wing its flight to a better

* Hon. Thomas Stevens, who died at Beverly the same day and nearly at the same time that Dr Abbot expired.

world. How readily does the character described in the text suggest the idea of that excellent, distinguished citizen, who has so long been an ornament and blessing of this community, and of this religious society. The general excellence of his character, the remarkable soundness of his judgment, the correctness of his opinions, and of his whole deportment; the great, extensive and propitious influence which he wielded, by which so much good resulted to this society, to the town and to the whole community, made his removal, a calamity of no ordinary character, an affliction which reaches every heart. O how dark are such dispensations of Providence in their first aspect! and how overwhelming the trial, had we no refuge to repair to. *The Lord God omnipotent reigneth:* and he reigns with perfect wisdom, rectitude and love. *Shall not the Judge of all the earth do right? Shall we receive good at the hands of the Lord and shall we not receive evil?* He leaves us the consolation of a good hope of those, who have lived in his fear and in his service. He leaves us the remembrance of the many excellences of their character, of the great good they have done. Their example is before us, as a pattern. The respect and love, with which while living they were regarded, and with which their memory is cherished, now they are dead, together with the glorious reward which awaits the righteous, are held out to us as most powerful inducements *to be followers* of those, who through faith and patience are inheriting the promises."

The following account of the formation of the First Church, in Beverly, and the settlement of the first minister, is extracted from the records of that Church :—

"The Lord in mercy alluring and bringing over into this wilderness of New England, many of his faithful servants from England, whose aim was to worship God in purity, according to his word: they, in pursuance of that work, began to set up particular Churches. And the first Church gathered in the Massachusetts Colony, was in this town of Salem ; a gracious beginning of that intended Church reformation which hath been further prosecuted and prospered through the Lord's mercy in divers parts of this land. This Church of Salem entered into church covenant, with fasting and prayer, upon the sixth day of the sixth month, [August 6,] 1629. Their number, at the beginning very small, was soon greatly increased, and enriched with divers worthy laborers in God's vineyard, as Pastors and Teachers, successively, viz : Mr Samuel Skelton, Mr Francis Higginson, Mr Hugh Peters, Mr Edward Norris, and Mr John Higginson, their present pastor.* As the Church increased, divers of the members came over the ferry to live on Bass River side, They on the tenth of the twelfth month, [February 10th] 1649, Mr Norris being Teacher, presented their request to the rest of the Church for some course to be taken for the means of grace amongst themselves, because of the tediousness and difficulties over the water, and other inconveniences ; which motion was renewed again the twenty second of the seventh month, [October 22d] 1650, and the second day of the eighth month they returned their answer, viz : That we should look out some able and approved Teacher to be amongst us, we still holding communion with them as before. But upon further experience, we upon the twenty third day of the first month, [March 23d] 1656,

* Mr ROGER WILLIAMS, who was a Minister in 1634 and 1635, is not noticed. He was expelled for some peculiarity of sentiment, and settled at Providence.

presented our desires to the church of ourselves, and after some agitation about it, when our Teacher stood for us, it was put to vote and consented unto, none appearing opposite, we protesting that there was no division of affection intended, but brotherly communion. Our desire being consented unto, we proceeded to build a Meeting House on Bass River side, and we called unto us successively, to dispense the word of life unto us, Mr Josiah Hubbard, Mr Jeremiah Hubbard, and Mr John Hale. After almost three years' experience of Mr John Hale, our motion was again renewed the twenty third day of the fourth month, [June 23d] 1667, and was as follows:—

We whose names are underwritten, the brethren and sisters belonging to Bass River, do present our desire to the members of the Church of Salem, that with their consent we and our children may be a Church of ourselves, and we also present unto Mr Hale, desiring him to join with us and to be our Pastor with the approbation of the members of the Church.

Roger Connant, Thomas Lathrop, William Dixey, Richard Dodge, Samuel Corning, Henry Herrick, William Woodberry, sen., William Dodge, sen., Humphrey Woodberry, sen., Robert Morgan, Peter Woolfe, Richard Brackenbury, Hugh Woodberry, John Black, sen., Josiah Rootes, sen., John Stone, sen., Nicholas Patch, Lott Conant, Exercise Conant, John Dodge, sen., John Hill, Ralph Ellingwood, Edward Bishop, Sarah Conant, Bethiah Lathrop, Anna Dixey, Mary Dodge, sen., Elizabeth Dodge, Elizabeth Corning, Anna Woodberry, sen., Elizabeth Woodberry, Ede Herrick, Elizabeth Haskell, Ellen Brackenbury, Anna Woodberry, jun., Mary Lovett, Martha Woolfe, Mary Dodge, jun., Mary Woodberry, Hannah Woodberry, Hannah Baker, Abigail Hill, Sarah Leach, Elizabeth Patch, Mary Herrick, Lydia Herrick, Freegrace Black, Hannah Gallowes, Bridget ———.

Such as are members, but not in full communion, desire to be dismissed with their parents. [Here follow twenty four names—the surnames the same as above, with two exceptions.]

This motion was answered the twenty first day of the fifth month, [July 21st] 1667, as follows viz. this writing being read, together with the names subscribed, there was a unanimous consent of the brethren present, unto their desire ; only it was left to the sacrament day after, when, in the fullest church assembly, the consent of the whole church was signified by their votes, and so they gave their liberty to be a Church of themselves, only they continued members here until their being a Church. The Lord grant his gracious presence with them."

On the 28th of August, 1667, the brethren renewed their call to Mr John Hale to be their Pastor, which he accepted. On the 20th of September following, they made confession of their faith and renewed their covenant, and proceeded to the ordination of Mr Hale, who was ordained by the laying on of hands of the Rev. John Higginson of Salem, Rev. Thomas Cobbett of Ipswich, and Rev. Antipas Newman of Wenham.

The town of Beverly was incorporated Oct. 14th, 1668.

Rev. John Hale died May 15th, 1700, in the sixty fourth year of his age.

Rev. Thomas Blowers was ordained Oct. 29th, 1701, and died June 17, 1729.

Rev. Joseph Champney was ordained on the second Wednesday of December, 1729, and died March 1st, 1773, in the sixty ninth year of his age.

Rev. Dr Joseph Willard was ordained in November, 1772, and dismissed by mutual consent, December, 1781, he having been appointed President of Harvard College. He died in 1804.

Rev. Dr Joseph McKean was ordained in March, 1785, and dismissed by mutual consent, August 23d, 1802, he having been appointed President of Bowdoin College. He died in 1807.

Rev. Dr Abiel Abbot was installed December 14th, 1803, and died June 7th, 1828, aged fifty eight.

In the space of one hundred and sixty one years, the Church and Society have enjoyed the ministry of six ministers with the greatest harmony. They have been destitute of a settled minister, during that period, for about six years in the whole.

Dr Abbot died on board the ship Othello, as she was entering the harbor of New York, from Charleston, South Carolina. He had been passing the cold season in Carolina, and in Cuba, for the benefit of his health, which was greatly improved; and he was hastening home to the circle of his friends, to the bosom of his family, and the flock of his charge. He arrived at Charleston, from the Havana, about the first of June. He preached at Charleston on Sunday, and on Monday embarked for New York, in good health and spirits. On Tuesday he was seized with a pain in his head, and continued ill for the remainder of the passage, though his case was not deemed dangerous. He was so well on Saturday morning as to dress himself and go upon deck, where he expired at half past twelve o'clock, just before the ship came to anchor at the Quarantine ground. His remains were deposited in the cemetery on Staten Island. The funeral services was performed by the Rev. Mr Miller.

■

www.ingramcontent.com/pod-product-compliance
Lightning Source LLC
Chambersburg PA
CBHW021550270326
41930CB00008B/1444